Sound and Light

Karen Bryant-Mole

Heinemann

First published in Great Britain by Heinemann Library, Halley Court, Jordan Hill, Oxford OX2 8EJ
a division of Reed Educational & Professional Publishing Ltd.

OXFORD FLORENCE PRAGUE MADRID ATHENS MELBOURNE AUCKLAND KUALA LUMPUR
SINGAPORE TOKYO IBADAN NAIROBI KAMPALA JOHANNESBURG GABORONE PORTSMOUTH
NH (USA) CHICAGO MEXICO CITY SAO PAULO

Designed by Jean Wheeler
Commissioned photography by Zul Mukhida
Consultant – Hazel Grice
Printed in Hong Kong

00 99 98
10 9 8 7 6 5 4 3 2

British Library Cataloguing in Publication Data

Bryant-Mole, Karen
Sound and light. - (Science all around me)
1. Light - Juvenile literature 2. Sound - Juvenile literature
I. Title
530

ISBN 0 431 07829 7

A number of questions are posed in this book. They are designed
to consolidate children's understanding by encouraging further
exploration of the science in their everyday lives.

**Words that appear in the text like this can
be found in the glossary.**

Acknowledgements
The Publishers would like to thank the following for permission to reproduce photographs. Chapel Studios 10, 14;
Eye Ubiquitous 4, 20; Positive Images 22; Tony Stone Images 6 (Nicole Katano), 8 (Mark Wagner), 12 (Tim Davis); Zefa 16, 18.

Every effort had been made to contact copyright holders of any material reproduced in this book. Any omissions will be
rectified in subsequent printings if notice is given to the Publisher.

Contents

What is sound?

A sound is made when something vibrates, or wobbles, very quickly.

The sound made by these musical instruments travels to the ears of the people all around.

Sounds make **liquid** in your ears vibrate. Your brain understands these vibrations as sounds.

? What is your favourite sound?

See for yourself ...

You can sometimes see objects vibrating as they make sounds.

Alex has put a plastic ruler under a book.
She uses one hand to hold down the book and the ruler.

She bends the other end of the ruler downwards.
When she lets go, the ruler will vibrate and make a sound.

High and low

Sometimes, things vibrate quickly.
Sometimes, they vibrate slowly.

The faster the wobble,
the higher the sound.
The slower the wobble,
the lower the sound.

When this violin makes
high sounds, its strings
vibrate quickly.

*Can you think of
anything that makes
a low sound?*

See for yourself ...

Aliyu has stretched a rubber band around an empty box.
He plucks the rubber band and watches it vibrate.

Aliyu has some more rubber bands of different lengths.
He is going to put them on his box.

He will find that the tighter the rubber band, the higher the sound it makes.

Loud and soft

Some sounds are soft.
Others are loud.

Leaves, rubbing together on the branches of trees make a soft sound.

This plane makes a very loud noise as it takes off.

? Can you think of anything else that makes a loud sound?

See for yourself ...

Whispers are very soft noises.
They are sometimes difficult to hear.

Yasmin and her friends are sitting in a circle.
Yasmin whispers a **sentence** to Kitty.
Kitty whispers what she hears to Maya and so on.

By the time it
gets back
to Yasmin,
the sentence
will probably
sound very
silly!

Sound makers

Sounds can be made by lots of different things.

Look at this picture.

The tape recorder
can play
story tapes.
The alarm clock
can ring.
The toy guitar
can be used to
make music.

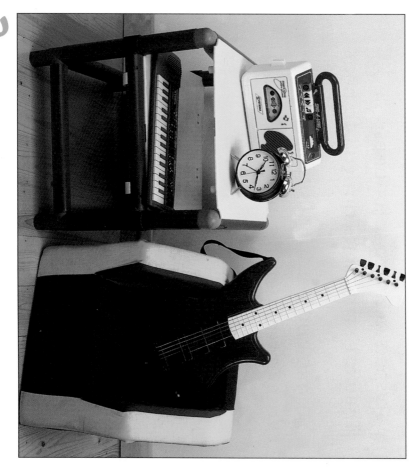

¿ Can you spot anything else that
makes a sound?

See for yourself ...

Alex has collected together some objects that make a noise.

She listens to each sound and decides whether it is high or low, loud or soft.

She is also trying to think of words, such as buzz, ding or hoot, that describe the sound each object makes.

Living things

People and animals make
sounds, too.
This dog can bark and yelp.

People can laugh and cry.
We put sounds together
in different ways to
make words.

We use words to talk
to each other.

*What sort of sound
would an angry dog make?*

See for yourself ...

We make sounds when special flaps of skin in our throat vibrates.

Sam has put his hand across the front of his throat.

When he puts his lips together and makes a low, humming sound, he can feel the vibrations through his hand.

Travelling sound

Every quarter of an hour, large bells inside this clock tower ring.

People living near the clock hear a very loud sound.

People living many streets away can hear the clock, too. But the sound they hear is much softer.

ⓘ The further you are from the **source** of a sound, the quieter it seems.

See for yourself ...

Leila has found a clock that ticks.

When she puts it to her ear,

the ticking sounds quite loud.

If she puts the clock
down on a table,
the ticking will sound
much quieter.

If she walks away
from the clock,
the ticking will
soon become
too quiet to hear.

What is light?

Light is a form of **energy**.

This bulb lights up when electricity flows through a thin wire inside the bulb. The wire heats up and makes a white light.

Objects that give out their own light can be called luminous.

i Televisions and computer screens are luminous, too.

See for yourself ...

Shiny objects sometimes look luminous, but really it is the light from something else bouncing off them.

Alex has put some objects on the table. Only one of the objects is luminous.

Sam is trying to work out which it is. Can you help him?

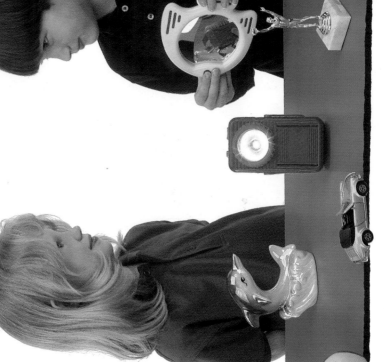

Sunlight

Can you see the rays of sunlight streaming through these trees?

Sunlight is a very important source of light.

We use sunlight to see by.
Plants need sunlight to grow.
All the food that we eat comes from plants, or from animals that eat plants.

See for yourself ...

Leila is eating a cheese sandwich.

The bread is made from wheat, which needs sunlight to grow.

The cheese and butter are made from milk, which comes from cows, who eat grass, which needs sunlight to grow.

How did sunlight help to make your last meal?

Darkness

Where there is no light, there is darkness. It is impossible to see anything in complete darkness.

This photograph was taken at night. Although it looks quite dark, it is not completely dark.

Moonlight and the lights in our homes and streets help us to see at night.

Planet Earth spins around. This gives us day and night.

See for yourself ...

Yasmin and Kitty are using a torch for the sun and a ball for Earth. Kitty has put a sticker on the ball to mark a place on Earth.

Yasmin shines the torch at the sticker. Kitty slowly spins the ball.

The sticker moves from 'day' to 'night'.

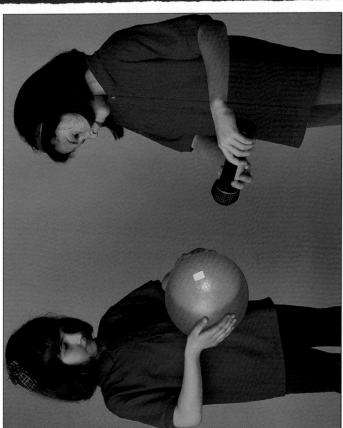

Shadows

Some things, such as air and glass, let light pass right through them.

Many things do not let light pass through them.
An area of darkness, or a shadow, is made behind them.

The wood, metal and string in this hammock do not let light through. But the air between them does.

What do you think made the other shadows in this picture?

See for yourself ...

Kitty is shining a beam of light from the torch onto a white wall.

Yasmin puts her hands between the torch and the wall.

She moves her hands to make funny shapes.

The light cannot pass through her hands.

A shadow is made that is the same shape as Yasmin's hands.

Glossary

energy what makes things work

liquid anything that can be
poured

plucks pulls up and lets go

sentence a group of words that
tells or asks something

source where something begins

travels moves from place to
place

Index